CW00427982

Tales from
Devon Folklore

James Whinray

Bossiney Books

This reprint 2018
First published 2014 by
Bossiney Books Ltd, 67 West Busk Lane, Otley, Leeds LS21 3LY
www.bossineybooks.com
ISBN 978-1-906474-43-0

Acknowledgement
The author and publishers are grateful to Tor Mark for permission
to use material first published in the author's *Devon Legends*
and *Devon Jokes and Stories*, both published in 1996

Printed in Great Britain by R Booth Ltd, Penryn, Cornwall

'Tales such as these flutter round Devon as plentifully as bats flit across the chimneys of an ancient manor house'

Arthur Norway, 1897

This book is based on *Devon Jokes and Stories* and *Devon Legends*, both by James Whinray, published by Tor Mark Press in 1996.

The stories were collected from many sources, among them Rev Sabine Baring-Gould, John Prince, Mrs Bray, John Aubrey, F J Snell, William Crossing, John Lloyd Warden Page, Sarah Hewett, Rev H J Whitfeld, Martin Dunsford and early volumes of the *Transactions of the Devonshire Association*.

Some are legends, others just anecdotes about famous Devon personalities. They are generally told in the original form, lightly edited to avoid archaic usages.

Kill'em or Cure'em Budd

Dr John Wreford Budd practised in Plymouth, one of an extensive medical family. He was a man of rough manners, blunt and to the point in all he said, and there are many anecdotes about him.

As a doctor, Budd broke through the wretched system that then prevailed of bleeding and giving lowering diet for every kind of malady. 'Chuck the slops away, and chuck the doctors after them, with their pills and lancets,' he thundered. 'Give the patient three or four glasses of champagne a day, a bowl of beef-tea every three hours, beefsteaks, mutton-chops and oysters.'

A small girl had a tiresome nervous cough. Dr Budd was called in. He heard her cough. Then he suddenly took her up in his arms and planted her on the mantleshelf.

'There!' said he. 'Balance yourself here for half an hour.' He pulled out his watch. 'If you cough, you will infallibly tumble over among the fire-irons and cut your head. You are a nice little girl, you are an active little girl, you are a pretty little girl; but you have one cussed fault which makes every one hate you, and I'm going to cure you of that. No coughing. The fire is burning, and if you do fall I suspect your skirt will catch fire, and you will be frightfully burnt, besides having your cheek cut open by the fender.'

Budd was visiting a farmer in the country. Every time he left, a prentice boy on the farm came with an anxious face to inquire how his master was. The doctor was touched at the intense interest the lad took in the condition of his master. One day as he left, and the boy asked after the farmer, Budd shook his head and said, 'I fear it's going bad with him.'

The lad burst into a loud boohoo of tears and sobs.

'There, there,' said the doctor, 'don't take on so, my lad. It can't be helped.'

'Oh, you'd take on if you were in my place,' sobbed the youth, 'for missus makes us eat all the stock, pigs and what not, as dies on the farm.'

Sir Walter's wooing

That great Devonian Sir Walter Raleigh was a favourite of Queen Elizabeth, but she liked her favourites to conceal discreetly any feelings they might have for other women, and Raleigh had to leave court when it became known that he had 'devirginated' one of the Queen's Maids of Honour, Elizabeth Throckmorton, whom he later married. The scurrilous John Aubrey (as ever) knew the details:

He loved a wench well; and one time getting one of the Maids of Honour up against a tree in a wood, who seemed at first boarding to be something fearful of her honour, and modest, she cried, 'Sweet Sir Walter, what do you ask me? Will you undo me? Nay, sweet Sir Walter! Sweet Sir Walter! Sir Walter!' At last as the danger and the pleasure at the same time grew higher, she cried in the ecstasy 'Swisser Swatter Swisser Swatter!' She proved with child, and I doubt not but this hero took care of them both, as also that the product was more than an ordinary mortal.

No smoking without fire

Sir Walter is said to have been the first man to introduce tobacco into England. When one of his servants first came into the room and, from behind, saw him apparently on fire, she threw a ewer of water over him to put it out.

Thicky's the way to Dartmoor

A famously disreputable family called Cheriton lived at Nymet Rowland. No one could beat them at rough horseplay and filthy language. They were a disgrace to their neighbourhood and a nuisance to their neighbours. One passer-by reported that he was accosted by a woman of the tribe who called him disgusting names, pelted him with mud and stones, performed indescribably offensive acts, and finally chased him with a hay fork, at which he beat a hasty retreat.

Their fame grew. Many inquisitive people went to Nymet Rowland to get a peep at the 'savages'. One man approached too near the house and was at once pounced upon by a couple of Amazons, who demanded the reason for his visit. 'Ladies,' said he, 'I have lost my way. Will you put me on the right road for Dartmoor?'

'Aw, eees, tü be sure,' replied Miss Cheriton, 'Come theäse yet way an' I'll shaw'ee.' She took him into the adjoining yard ostensibly to direct him, but the unsuspecting wayfarer, venturing too near the edge of the horse pond in following his guide, was suddenly thrust into the filthy liquid, as a 'There, thicky's the way tü Dartymoor, and be damned tü you,' fell on his ears.

The Mayor of Bradninch returns an answer

In the time when eating and drinking were the chief duties of civic office, a mayor of Exeter sent a polite letter to his counterpart in Bradninch, by special messenger, inviting him to dine. The messenger found his worship of Bradninch on the roof of a house, following his calling as a thatcher. On being informed that there was a note for him, he asked the messenger to bring it up the ladder.

His worship, not being able to read, and there being no town clerk present, opened it and held it before him, pretending to read, and considering what reply to make whilst not knowing the contents or even whom it was from. The messenger, observing that the letter was being held upside down, humbly hinted as much to the mayor. His worship immediately replied, 'How dare you, you impertinent scoundrel, dictate to the Mayor of Bradninch in what way he shall read a letter? Go home to your master, and tell him that when he sends a more discreet and civil messenger, I'll return him an answer.'

To which of you am I betrothed?

The Tremaine family, of Sydenham House near Marystow, not infrequently included twins. At one time, there were two identical girls, one of whom had been on a visit to a friend in the country, where she had won the heart of a young gentleman, who soon became her accepted lover. It was of course necessary for him to obtain her father's consent, and for this purpose he followed her to London. On his arrival, he was shown into a room where the other sister, whom he had never seen, was sitting alone; instantly mistaking her for his betrothed, he addressed her as such.

The young lady, who had a mind to keep up the joke, let him continue for a few minutes, when the door opened and in came the other twin. The lover, astonished to find two sweethearts where he expected but one, and not knowing which was the right one, felt himself under the necessity of begging they would be kind enough to tell him to which lady he was engaged.

The voyage of Cove's bed

In 1537 a flood swelled the Exe so much that in the middle of the night the torrent destroyed a pier of the bridge at Tiverton. Right alongside the bridge was the house of a man named Cove, and as the bridge collapsed it took Cove's house along with it. It was a three storey house and it fell with a great crash; the servants in topmost rooms were all thrown into the river and drowned, but Cove and his wife, sleeping in a lower room, were carried into the water, bed and all. He ordered his wife not to rock the boat, and using sometimes his hands and sometimes his feet instead of oars, kept himself on the west side of the river, out of a strong eddy, and at length reached a hillock where the waters were shallow, and he and his wife came ashore safely.

Coffin leaps into grave

The vicars of Bideford were entitled to claim a 'heriot', or death duty, whenever a farmer in the parish died, and this was to consist of the dead man's best cow. This dubious custom probably dated back even before William the Conqueror granted Bideford to the son of Hamo the Toothy.

Sir William Coffin (whose descendants are now the Pine-Coffins) was passing the churchyard one day in 1529 when he observed a commotion. A corpse was awaiting burial. The priest would not bury it until he had received his heriot, but the dead man had possessed only one cow and no other property, so his widow and children would become destitute. After unsuccessfully trying to reason with the greedy priest, Sir William leapt into the grave, saying to the priest, 'Very well, then, stick me in the grave and cover me up, instead of the corpse; and you can have my second best cow.'

At this the priest thought it might be safer to yield – yet afterwards he complained to the ecclesiastical court and Sir William was charged with violating the privileges of the church. But his court contacts were such that he not only escaped punishment, he even persuaded parliament to improve the law by abolishing such heriots.

Another version of this story says that Sir William put the priest in the grave and almost buried him alive. Take your pick!

The workhouse is where you lay your head

In the days when each parish was responsible for its own paupers, there were many shabby attempts to pass paupers from one parish to another, and as a result many unfortunate men and women suffered even greater hardship than if they had been accepted into their nearest workhouse.

One such dispute, however, had its amusing aspect. Hornshayne House, the home of the Marwood family in the eighteenth century, was situated on the junction of the parish boundaries of Colyton, Southleigh and Farway. In 1765, a servant at the house became a pauper – probably because he could no longer work through age or sickness. Which parish should support him? Colyton was able to claim that only the Hornshayne dairy was in their parish, and the man had not worked in the dairy, so they were not responsible. So it was between Southleigh and Farway. Their lawyers were finally able to agree that the crucial point was where he slept – but his bed lay across the boundary! Back it went to the lawyers, who declared that in such a case the crucial point was where he laid his head to sleep, so two arbitrators went to the house.

It was clear where the parish boundary ran, because in those days 'beating the bounds' was an annual ritual, and every boy in the area knew that the boundary went along the line of a beam through the Hornshayne kitchen. But the servant had his bed in the garret, so surveyors were called in to plot a true perpendicular line from his pillow (once they had taken depositions as to which was the head of the bed and which the foot) down to the kitchen.

And whilst Southleigh had him from the chest downwards, it appeared that Farway had the honour of his head – and so Farway had to maintain him. But they probably spent less in doing so than they had already spent on lawyers' fees.

Stories of the hunting parsons

At the beginning of the nineteenth century, few counties in England produced such a crop of hunting parsons as did Devonshire.

Parson Jack Russell was said to be 'a worthy, kind-hearted, God-fearing man,' and our attitude towards him will depend largely on our attitude to hunting, and to the yappy little brutes to which he gave his name! Perhaps he did spend most of his time in the chase, and rather too little at his job, but his flock liked him and he did live among them, which is more than can be said for many of his contemporaries.

Parsons Froude and Radford were in a different league entirely. They were both undoubtedly guilty of serious crimes, for which they were never brought to justice. Here are some stories about the three of them, and of Bishop Phillpotts who was consecrated Bishop of Exeter in 1831.

Brotherly love

A dispute arose between Parsons Froude and Russell, stemming from some uncharitable words in the field.

Froude was not the kind of man to 'pass by a matter' even if he were ever so much in the wrong, and the opportunity arose on the way home of trying to vindicate at least his seniority – for he was an older man than Russell. They met again at the top of the narrow lane that leads from Court Down to Dulverton – a very lonely spot with high hedges on either side completely shutting out and shutting in all views and sounds. As his powerful nag was trotting stoutly down through the mud, making loud suction noises with his hooves and spurting up the dirty water on every side, Russell saw Froude ahead of him, dismounted, with his weedy thoroughbred drawn right across the lane, completely blocking his way, and he guessed it foreboded evil. As he drew near, 'Who'th a-made thee into a lecturing Beeshop like mi lord Veel-the-Pot of Exeter, I should like vor knaw?' began Froude. 'While thee's a-got they there blaggard rascals about thee and a vew of the gintry thee canst zay 'at thee'st like I s'pose. 'Tis my turn now! Git off thick there gurt cart 'oss o'thine and I'll taich thee better manners!'

'I will certainly obey you,' replied Russell (getting off his horse and tying his reins to a stump in the hedge), 'since you are my senior by ten years at least. What now?' he added, and turned round and faced him. As he did so, Froude's hunting crop fell in a heavy blow over his shoulder, leaving his ear bleeding and his back tingling from the smartest cut he had ever received since he was at Blundell's School. But the next moment he had gripped the striker, wrested the weapon from his hands, thrown it aside and, with what was among wrestlers called a Lancashire twist, had laid Froude gently and impotently on his back upon the Autumn grass, holding both arms down by the sides and bestriding his legs to keep him from kicking.

How long he would have held him there I do not know, for his task was to keep him in this position until he got into a better temper and on his honour promised to proceed in a peaceable way and acknowledge that the rebuke he had given him was just and right.

But while he was reasoning with him thus, face to face, another hunter came trotting down the lane. When he saw the two horses tied to the hedge, and then looked upon the two parsons, the one struggling and fuming and swearing on the ground, and the other kneeling over his victim and arguing with him in the kindest language, he first of all burst into laughter, and then, when he saw the angry looks of Jack Froude, and Russell's bleeding face: 'Gentlemen, gentlemen!' said he. 'What be you about here? – two brethren of the cloth! Two deputies of peace and good will amongst men! Fighting like two ruffians on the highway! Like two stags in the rutting season! Like two ill-behaved hounds in the hunting field! What would Bishop Phillpotts say if he saw ye now? But if neither of ye would take heed to him – so let me tell ye that Mr Bisset and Lord Ebrington are coming on behind with a number of others, and what a disgrace it will be for them to see you like this! How delighted the Radical papers will be to publish a column with this title, "Two parsons fighting on the Highway!"'

With that Froude gave way and yielded all the other asked him to yield, and they both rose to their feet just as a large party of riders came down the lane. 'What's the matter, Parson Froude?' said

Mr Bisset, as they passed. 'Ah! I thought that weedy toad of a horse would come down with ye!'

Froude did not answer.

'Yes,' said Russell, 'but it might have been much worse, Mr Bisset – much worse – much worse! 'Twas an easy fall!'

And then they all laughed together as they rode on – except Froude, and he rode away silent, with the mud still hanging to his red coat and hat.

Unprepare ye the way of the Lord Bishop

On one occasion Bishop Phillpotts planned a visit to Froude, vicar of Knowstone and a man who ruled his locality with a gang of ruffians, who thought nothing of firing a rick at his suggestion, or loosening a carriage wheel so that the driver was spilled.

Froude had no wish to see the bishop, so he had the road dug up. A wide hole was created, into which a marsh would drain. It was covered lightly with turf and a layer of dust, and the bishop drove straight into it. He realised it was no accident, but persisted on foot. When he arrived, the reception was chilly, but he was offered a drink. He declined, and Froude helped himself to a large one. The bishop opened the conversation.

'I hear, Mr Froude, that you keep a pack of harriers.'

'Then you hear wrong, my lord. It is the pack that keeps me.'

'I do not understand.'

'They stock my larder with hares. You don't suppose I should have hares on my table unless they were caught for me? There's no butcher for miles and miles, and I can't get a joint but once in a fortnight. Forced to eat hares. And they must be caught to be eaten.'

The Bishop then said to Froude, 'I hear, sir, but I can hardly credit it, that you invite men to your house and keep them drinking and then fighting in your parlour.'

'My lord, you are misinformed. Don't believe a word of it. Directly they begins to fight and takes off their coats, I take 'em by the scruff of the neck and turns them out into the churchyard, and let 'em settle their differences among the tombs.'

Your lover or your pig?

Froude agreed to give his housekeeper a pig if she would give up her sweetheart, and continue to work for him. 'Which will you prefer now, Joe or the porker?' 'Lauk, sir, I'd rayther have the pig.'

But Froude suspected her of having her bacon and eating it, and one day he deliberately returned home unexpectedly when Joe was in the kitchen. Where to hide him? Where else, but in the great 'copper' used for laundry. Froude came into the room and looked about him. Something about the copper made him suspicious. On a pretext, he made his housekeeper fill the copper, pouring the water all over Joe, and then he made her light the fire, and stayed to watch. Joe bore it as manfully as a missionary in a cooking pot, but in the end there was no alternative but to leap out and make a dash for it.

With a wild hunting cry, Froude made after him with his horse-whip.

Mrs Russell's hounds

When Parson Jack Russell was over eighty he started keeping a pack of harriers. The Bishop of Exeter sent for him.

'Mr Russell, I hear you have got a pack of hounds. Is it so?'

'It is. I won't deny it , my lord.'

'Well, Mr Russell, it seems to me rather unsuitable for a clergy-man to keep a pack. I do not ask you to give up hunting, for I know it would not be possible for you to exist without that. But will you, to oblige me, give up the pack?'

'Do y'ask it as a personal favour, my lord?'

'Yes, Mr Russell, as a personal favour.'

'Very well then, my lord, I will.'

'Thank you, thank you.' The Bishop, moved by his readiness, held out his hand. 'Give me your hand, Mr Russell; you are – you really are – a good fellow.'

Jack Russell gave his great fist to the Bishop, who pressed it warmly. As they stood thus hand in hand, Jack said –

'I won't deceive you, not for the world, my lord. I'll give up the pack sure enough – but Mrs Russell will keep it instead of me.'

The Bishop dropped his hand.

Horse trading

Russell thought that in horse dealing, as in love and war, all things are lawful. It so happened that Parson Froude wanted a horse, and he asked his dear friend Russell if he knew where he could find one that was suitable. 'Would my brown horse do?' asked Russell. 'I want to sell him, because the hunting season is over and I have too many horses. Come into town on Saturday and dine with me in the middle of the day, and see the horse. If you like him, you can have him, and if you do not, there is no harm done.'

On Saturday, into South Molton came Froude. Russell lived there, as he was then curate of nearby George Nympton. Froude stabled his horse at the lower end of the town. He was suspicious even of a friend, so, instead of going to Russell's lodging, he went to his stable and found the door locked. This circumstance made him more suspicious than ever, and, looking round, he saw a man on a ladder, from which he was thatching a cottage. He called to him for assistance, shifted the ladder to the stable, ascended and went by the 'tallet' door into the loft. He got down the steps inside, opened the window, and carefully inspected the horse, which he found to be suffering in both eyes from incipient cataract.

He climbed back, got down the ladder, and shutting the window, went into a shop to have his coat brushed before he rang his friend's door-bell. The door was opened by Russell himself, who saluted him with: 'You are early Froude, come across to the bank with me for a moment, if you do not mind.'

In the street was standing a Combe Martin cart laden with early vegetables, and between the shafts was an old pony, stone blind, with glassy eyeballs. Froude paused, lifted the pony's head, turned its face to the light, looked at the white eyeballs and remarked, 'How blessed plenty blind horses there are in this town just now, Jack.'

Not another word was said. The dinner was eaten, the bottle of port wine was consumed, and Froude rode home without having been asked to see the brown horse. Russell knew the game was up, and that his little plan for making his friend view the horse after he had dined, and not before, had lamentably failed.

But that was the way with them. Froude would have dealt with his best friend in the same manner over horses.

Time, gentlemen, please

The rector of Peter Tavy, the Rev Mr McBean, would not start the morning service until he was sure that none of the villagers were in the pub, which was right next to the churchyard. He used to send the churchwarden out to check on this. Now the churchwarden was a relative of the landlord, so his position was a delicate one. Being a man of peace, he hit upon a solution. As he walked across the churchyard, with his eyes fixed on the ground immediately in front of his toes, he repeated, getting louder as he approached, 'I'm coming, Cousin Tom, I'm coming, Cousin Tom.' At the door of the pub he would check that it was empty of customers – which it always was – and return to the church to report that the sermon could start. The vicar congratulated himself on his parishioners having such regard for the hours of worship.

Counting her chicks

Sir Lewis Pollard was a judge in Tudor times, and often obliged to be away from his home at King's Nympton. He left his wife in charge of preparing a stained glass window in the church, in which the couple were to appear accompanied by their children – of whom at the time there were no less than twenty-one. Lady Pollard, however, decided to have twenty-two children depicted, presuming that when her husband returned, there would be time for one more. Which, as Prince, the author of *Devon Worthies* says, 'inserted in expectation, came to pass in reality'.

Honi soit qui mal y pense

Prince Charles, later King Charles II, spent several weeks as a fugitive after the Royalist defeat at the Battle of Worcester. It was during this time that he escaped discovery by hiding in an oak tree. But he is said to have had an even narrower escape when, closely pursued, he sought refuge at Coaxdon House, near Axminster. Entering the parlour where the lady of the house, Mrs Cogan, was alone, he threw himself on her protection. It was then the fashion for ladies to wear large hoops, and as there was no time to be lost and the soldiers were even then entering the grounds, she instantly concealed him under her skirt.

Mrs Cogan was a royalist, but her husband was one of the opposite party, and was then out in his estate. When he saw the soldiers approaching the house, he joined them and they all walked into the room in which the lady was sitting, she affecting surprise at their intrusion. The men immediately announced their business, stating that as Prince Charles must be concealed upon the premises, they were authorised to make a strict search for him. Assenting with apparent readiness to their object, Mrs Cogan kept her seat while her husband accompanied them through every room in the house.

Being released from the immediate predicament, she was then able to provide for the security of the fugitive until it was prudent for him to depart, and furnished him with provisions and a change of clothes. He then left, and made his way to what was then the poor fishing village of Brighthelmstone, now Brighton, and thence to France.

When in safety, Charles unsurprisingly remembered the incident, and sent her a handsome gold chain and locket. The Order of the Garter would perhaps have been more appropriate.

There be a hand here as can strike

Another escape story of the Civil War concerns Henry Bidlake. Cromwell's troops surrounded Bidlake House, in order to capture him, but he was tipped off, and dressed himself in rags in order to pass them. Some of the soldiers met him, and asked whether he had seen Squire Bidlake. 'Aye, sure,' he replied, ''er was a-standin' on 's own doorstep a foo minutes agoo.'

So they went on to search the house, while he escaped to the house of a tenant named Veale in Burleigh Wood. The troopers went there also, and Mrs Veale made him slide into the clock-case. They hunted high and low but could not find him. One of the soldiers, looking at the clock and seeing the hand at the hour, said 'What, doant he strike?' 'Aye, aye, mister,' replied Mrs Veale, 'there be a hand here as can strike, I tell 'ee.'

Mr Bidlake suffered from a chronic cough, and just at that moment he had the art to dip his head and let the weight down behind his back, so that the clock struck the hour and drowned the cough in the case.

Richard is himself again

The great actor Edmund Kean played in 'rep' at a theatre in Exeter before he became famous, and in his spare time taught fencing and elocution. The arty crowd of Exeter in his day congregated at the Turk's Head, in a room along a passage.

Kean is said to have left Exeter on foot, and returned in a coach and horses, but he had not forgotten his old friends. He ordered his coach to stop at the inn door, ran along the passage, burst into the room and, quoting his most famous part, Richard III, leaped onto the table declaiming 'Richard's himself again!'

Practical clockmanship

On an outlying farm the clock went wrong, and struck one at three, and two at four, and so on. This was a nuisance, as people were unable to remember which was wrong, the hands or the chimes. But the farmer settled it by keeping the clock an hour fast, and then, when it pointed to one and struck eleven, everyone knew it was twelve.

An appetite for news

An old woman of seventy-five was to be photographed by an amateur. Nothing he said could persuade her to speak till the operation was completed. Then she put her finger into her mouth: 'You wouldn't ha' me took wi' my cheeks falled in? I just stuffed the *Western Marnin' News* in my mouth to fill'n out.'

The stuff of which ghosts are made

A dining club used to meet at the 'Bunch of Grapes' in Kinterbury Street, Plymouth, and their president was one Humphrey Tallent. One evening his chair was all too conspicuously empty, for he was lying at death's door. There was a general air of gloom in the normally convivial meeting, when suddenly the door flew open and a spectre, pale and ghastly, and dressed in dressing gown and night-cap, entered, and sat on a footstool. The company was speechless, until one, braver than the rest, ventured to say, 'I am glad to see you here again, sir. I hope you are better?'

The apparition only bowed, raised an empty glass and moved its lips in the toast of death, and withdrew, as silently as it had entered. When the general shock had passed, one of the members walked across to Mr Tallent's house, to enquire after his health and learned to his horror that he had just died. The faith of the members that they had seen his spirit at the point of his death was unshaken – until the nurse confessed that she fell asleep while attending the dying man, and found when she woke that he had left the room. A few minutes later, he returned from the club, composed himself, and, exhausted by the effort, breathed his last.

Snails house

Below Lough Tor (Laughter Tor on Ordnance Survey maps) is a cottage once known as White Slade, but nicknamed Snails House in Victorian times. Here there lived two spinsters, plump and healthy, but with no visible means of subsistence. No food was ever seen to enter their door, and they kept no poultry or livestock. Dark suspicions arose. How did these ladies live? Was it on Dartmoor mutton, stolen and brought to the house at dead of night? So a posse of moor-folk visited the house, and strangely they were admitted willingly to make a search. For a time nothing edible could be found – then, triumph! – certain pans were discovered and dragged forth excitedly. Disappointment! Salted slugs!

But curiously, after this the two ladies gradually pined away, till there were no more miserable-looking creatures upon the moor.

Dissenters' plot

A vicar of Talaton hated dissenters. He heard that a plot of land in the village was for sale, and that the dissenters were after it to build a chapel, so he bought it himself at a high price. News of this got around, and whenever any piece of land came on the market it was rumoured that the dissenters were after it. The rector and his purse rose to every occasion…

Wheel that boat!

When George Monk, later Duke of Albemarle and the key figure in the restoration of the Stuarts, first took employment under Oliver Cromwell, it was at sea against the Dutch. He had previously been a cavalry officer under Charles I. He performed good service, and was courageous enough, but he distinguished no better between the armed services than between rulers: instead of crying 'Tack about,' he would shout 'Wheel to the right!'

A snow white cloth

The village of Lydford was much neglected by its landlord and by its pluralist vicar. A poor curate officiated there, on a salary of £100 a year. One Christmas Day, the curate went to the church to celebrate Holy Communion and found the altar covered with snow that had blown in through the battered east window and under the cracked slates of the roof.

'I'll sweep it off,' said the clerk.

'On no account. God has spread his table,' said the curate; and he celebrated on the white sheet of snow.

After the PM's neck

Lord North, then a far from popular Prime Minister, was staying at Ashe at harvest time in 1765. He heard from a neighbouring field the reapers 'crying the neck', and saw them waving their sickles in the air.

Not knowing of this ancient custom, when the reapers dedicated the last sheaf to the spirit of the harvest, he was convinced that they were after his own neck.

His fears were communicated to his friend Sir Robert Hamilton, who drew his sword and rushed into the midst of the astonished labourers. The misunderstanding was soon sorted out and the sword returned bloodless to its scabbard.

Ironically, Lord North's instinct may have been correct, for it is conjectured that the ancient custom may be the relic of a human sacrifice, where the first passing stranger was seized and killed to propitiate the gods.

A unique event

The parson of Blackborough announced to his sparse congregation that if they would come to church next Sunday, they would see something they had never seen before in their lives. They came, and the rest of the parish came, and he remarked that neither he nor they had ever seen their church so full.

One may doubt whether it was ever full again afterwards.

Another dish of tay?

Dr Johnson visited Plymouth, and was much impressed, both by the naval dockyard and the local produce. One day he indulged so heavily at dinner in honey, clotted cream and new cider that his friends feared for his life. But the man who could drink nineteen cups of tea (at a time when it cost two guineas a pound) was hardly likely to restrain himself over such homely luxuries as honey, cream and cider.

It is said that his hostess ironically asked him whether he would care for the twentieth cup. As the Doctor gruffly responded in the affirmative, she rang the bell and told the servant to bring a bucket from the stable.

Such was his renown that a local alderman came to consult him on an important question. The 'Dockers', or inhabitants of the town which was then called Dock and is now Devonport, were suffering from a drought, and were pleading to be allowed some of Plymouth's excess water. The alderman showed by the way he put the question that he opposed allowing this, and Dr Johnson, with heavy irony, replied, 'I'd let the rogues die of thirst, for I hate a Docker from my heart.'

The alderman joyfully reported back to the his Council colleagues that the great Dr Johnson shared his opinion entirely.

Winstanley's wish come true

When Henry Winstanley, 'the Merlin of his age', was building his fanciful and audacious lighthouse on the Eddystone rock, England was at war with France. A French privateer surprised the working party, while the ship which should have protected them (the aptly named HMS *Terrible*) was neglecting its duties. The French took a few pot-shots for amusement, then landed and took Winstanley captive, although they left the workmen.

When King Louis found out, he was horrified and ordered Winstanley released immediately. He said he was 'at war with England and not with humanity', and apologised in person to the inventor.

Winstanley was a genius at self-publicising, and this incident was a gift. Before long everyone in England had heard of the obscure but lethal reef.

The light was lit on 14 November 1698. The outside of the lighthouse was already festooned with cranes and ornamental candelabra, but Winstanley had added 'a moving engine trough to cast down stones to defend the landing stage in case of need'. However, he had reckoned without HMS *Terrible*, which press-ganged the only boatman in Plymouth able and willing to land supplies on the rock, so the keepers nearly starved before he could effect the man's release.

Winstanley had total confidence in his pioneering structure, and expressed the wish to be in it 'during the greatest storm that ever was'. By chance, he was. The storm of 26 November 1703 was a misplaced hurricane which did incredible damage across the whole of England. On land, it totally destroyed a thousand or more houses and four hundred windmills. At sea, the Royal Navy alone lost thirteen ships, many smaller craft, and some two thousand men drowned. Winstanley and his keepers were swept away, and there was scarcely any trace of the building by the time the storm blew itself out.

Taking the lead

The second Eddystone lighthouse lasted rather longer than Winstanley's, and was destroyed by fire rather than by storm, in 1755. One of the surviving keepers was aged 94. After being burned in the fire, then awaiting rescue on the wave-swept rock for several hours and finally – because it was too rough to land a boat – being dragged off through the waves on a rope's end, he was thought to have lost his wits when he claimed to have accidentally swallowed some of the molten lead from the roof. He appeared to be recovering, then suddenly relapsed after twelve days, and died. Had he really swallowed lead after all? The doctor knew only one way to find out. An autopsy revealed in his stomach a flat piece of lead weighing 200 grams, and over ten centimetres across.

A living proportionable to his mind

The Earl of Devon gave the substantial rectory of Tiverton to his chaplain, who lived for some time there on its income, but well beyond his means. He would complain to his lord's officers about his general lack of money, and sometimes more specifically, that the living did not produce the income needed to entertain in a style appropriate to someone of his standing.

As he spoke often in this way, it came to the attention of the Earl, who invited his former chaplain to come and discuss his complaint. He told the parson that he had considered the matter and that he intended 'to procure him a living more proportionable to his mind and convenience', if at some stage he would first care to resign his present living.

The incumbent, encouraged by these words and in the hope of higher promotion, handed in his immediate resignation. Whereupon the Earl explained that he intended to divide the living of Tiverton into four parts, Prior, Tidcombe, Clare and Pitt, and to bestow these smaller livings on four separate men. But out of respect to his former chaplain, and former incumbent, he would offer him the first choice. Seeing his lordship's intent, and being without any other great connection from which he might hope for preferment, he accepted gratefully, 'and thereby was fairly taught to live by a crown who could not live by a pound.'

No modern HR director could have managed it better.

Devon's old roads

When the first Turnpike Act in Devon was applied for, its proposer in the Commons said it would in fact be no more expensive to make the roads navigable under a Navigation Act than to make them fit for carriages under a Turnpike Act, so much water already lay in them.

Espionage

In the 1740s, Tiverton, formerly a major cloth manufacturing town, began to lose its main Dutch market. This was not because of the industrial revolution, which had not then got fully under way, but because the type of coarse cloth produced in Tiverton was held in lower esteem than new types of cloth produced in Norwich – 'camblets, tarborates, damasks, barragons, lutestrings, calamancoes, tarbines' and other exotic stuffs. Men were laid off and factories closed in Tiverton, and it led to riots and tumults in the town, especially when Irish wool was imported and the wool-combers lost their livelihood.

One of the leading firms was that of Mrs Enchmarch & Sons (for there were many successful businesswomen in the eighteenth century) and Mrs Enchmarch sent one of her sons to Norwich, with a weaver named William Perkins. They remained there some time to make themselves fully acquainted with the plans of the woollen manufacturers there. They had almost completed their industrial espionage when their purpose was suspected, and it was with great difficulty and hazard that they escaped from the city. Had they fallen into the hands of their pursuers, it would probably have cost them their lives.

The jester's view of hell

John Arscott of Tetcott (1718-1783) was a country squire of the kind described by Fielding in *Tom Jones*. He kept possibly the last dwarf jester in England, Black John. One evening Black John fell asleep by the hearth in the hall at Tetcott. Suddenly he started up with a cry, 'Oh, master, I was in a sog [sleep] and I thought I was dead and in hell.'

'Well, John,' said the squire, 'and what did you see there?'

'Sir, everything very much like what it is here in Tetcott Hall, the gentlefolks nearest the fire.'

Coming up trumps

A vicar of Moreton was playing whist one evening in a country house when he had a heart attack while dealing. The standard

Edwardian remedies were applied, hartshorn, burnt feathers, and so on, and he recovered. Everybody looked at him, as people do in such circumstances, perhaps waiting for some word of the great beyond. 'What's trumps?' he asked quietly.

Daughter Olive

When Cecil Torr (who wrote the wonderfully entertaining *Small Talk at Wreyland*) found that some of his neighbours had never seen olives, he gave them some from the tree in his garden. One commented, 'Well, Mrs —'d never have christened her daughter Olive, if her'd a-tasted one of they.'

The humbling church

Richard Polwhele comments in his *History of Devonshire* that the inhabitants of Brent Tor, where the church is on top of a steep 300 metre high hill, make weekly atonement for their sins: for they can never go to church without the previous penance of climbing up this steep hill, which they are often obliged to attempt, in the lowliest attitude. In windy or rainy weather, the worthy pastor himself is frequently obliged to humble himself on all fours, preparatory to his being exalted in the pulpit.

Rural devil

There is a famous story that the devil destroyed Widecombe church when he caught a sinner napping (the church was dramatically struck by lightning in 1638 during a service) and that the devil had stopped on his way across the moor to Widecombe and asked for water at a remote cottage. A woman living in that same cottage two hundred years later saw a tall man dressed in black, on a great black stallion, loom out of the fog, and ask for water. It was in fact the rural dean, but she fled before discovering this. She said it was his horns which had convinced her.

Church losses

For centuries people have been gradually deserting the church of England, often for doctrinal reasons, but not always. One elderly lady did so because her grandchild had caught its death of cold through the parson 'a-baptizin' it without a-puttin' a kettleful o' bilin' water into that stoney font.'

The nutty ghost

Old Mother Elston used to go from place to place selling nuts, and before she died she begged that a bag of them should be put in her coffin. Her wishes were fulfilled when she was buried. Then it began to be said that her ghost used to sit on her grave and crack nuts. Many people had heard it, and the clergyman of the parish was told. He said that if at any time its presence was made known to him, he would come at once and lay it.

One fine night, after a neighbouring 'revel' [parish feast day], three men rather the worse for drink came by, and saw some sheep in a field close to the churchyard. The thought struck them that this was a good opportunity for helping themselves. While one man went to the porch to keep watch, the others went off to steal the sheep. Now the man in the porch had brought a lot of nuts from the revel, and while waiting he began to eat them. Just then, the sexton came by, heard the nuts being cracked and immediately ran to the vicarage to fetch the parson, who agreed to come at once.

Unfortunately he was afflicted with St Vitus' Dance and could not walk, being dependent on a wheelchair. But the wheelchair could not immediately be found.

'Never mind, for this little distance you can carry me on your back,' said the parson. So off they went and just inside the church-yard they heard the nuts still being cracked. The sexton stopped. 'Go a little nearer,' said the parson. The sexton went a little nearer. 'A little nearer still,' he urged and the sexton edged closer. Then the parson began to speak some words to lay the ghost.

But the man in the porch, seeing the silhouette of the vicar on the sexton's shoulders, thought it was one of his mates returning with a sheep. 'Is he fat?' he called. The sexton was so frightened that he dropped the parson and ran away as fast as he could. But just as fright brings on St Vitus' Dance, so it can cure it, and from that time the vicar could walk as well as ever he could.

The Doones of Bagworthy

In 1869, R D Blackmore's novel *Lorna Doone* was published, and promptly gave Exmoor publicity and notoriety. The story was at first thought to be his own invention, but a little guidebook to Lynton and Lynmouth, published about fifteen years earlier, reveals an older tradition. Whether Blackmore used this book as his inspiration, or had the story direct, is not known.

Here is the old story:

Bagworthy, or Badgeworthy as it is called by the peasants, lies on the side of Brendon parish adjoining Somersetshire, and connected with this spot are various traditions of the doings of a daring and successful band of robbers called 'the Doones of Bagworthy' who seem to have taken up their residence there about the time of the Commonwealth. Situated among the extensive tracts of hills which surround Exmoor, far from the habitation of man, and until its enclosure in 1820 scarcely known to any but the half barbarous shepherd or the adventurous sportsman, stands the wood of Bagworthy.

Though still one of the favourite haunts of the forest deer, the stately natives of the glen and mountains, it has been decreasing in size for many years; and its boundaries half a century ago, as pointed out by some of the older shepherds, by far exceed its present dimensions.

The ruins of a village long forsaken and deserted stand in an adjacent valley, which before the destruction of the timber must have been a spot entirely suited to the wild inhabitant. Tradition relates that it consisted of eleven cottages, and that here the 'Doones' took up their residence, being the terror of the country for many miles around. For a long time they were in the habit of escaping with their booty across the wild hills of Exmoor to Bagworthy, where few thought it safe or even practicable to follow them. They were not natives of this part of the country, but having been stirred by the Revolution from their homes, suddenly entered Devonshire and erected the village alluded to. It was known from the first, to the inhabitants of the neighbouring parishes, that this village was erected and inhabited by robbers, but the fear which their deeds inspired in the minds of the peasants prevented them from attacking and destroying it. The idea is prevalent that before leaving home they had been men of distinction and not common peasants. The site of a house may still be seen on a part of the forest, called the Warren, which is said to have belonged to a person styled 'The Squire', who was robbed and murdered by the Doones.

A farm-house called Yenworthy, lying just above Glenthorne on the left of the Lynton and Porlock road, was beset by them one night; but a woman firing on them from one of the windows with a long duck gun, they retreated, and blood was tracked the next morning for several miles in the direction of Bagworthy. The gun was later found at Yenworthy, and purchased by the Rev W S Halliday. They entered and robbed a house at Exford in the evening before dark, and found there a child, whom they murdered; a woman servant who had concealed herself in the oven is said to have heard them say to the unfortunate infant the following barbarous couplet:

'If any one asks, who kill'd thee,
Tell them, 'twas the Doones of Bagworthy.'

It was for this murder that the whole county rose in arms against them, and going to their abode in great haste and force, succeeded in taking into custody the whole gang, who soon after met with the punishment due to their crimes.

Faggus and his strawberry horse

Faggus was a native of North Molton and by trade a blacksmith, but being engaged in a law suit with Sir Richard Bampfylde, he was ruined and obliged to leave his home. He then turned gentleman robber, and for many years collected contributions on the highways, sometimes with a companion named Penn, but more frequently alone.

Many stories are now told concerning his enchanted strawberry horse, that rescued him from all sorts of dangers, and it was chiefly by means of this horse that Faggus escaped punishment for so great a length of time.

On one occasion a large party of farmers agreed to ride home together from Barnstaple Fair, expressly for the purpose of avoiding an attack from Faggus, who was supposed to be in the neighbourhood.

However, when they arrived at the post on the top of Bratton Down, Faggus rode up, a cocked pistol in each hand and the reins lying on the neck of his strawberry horse. He threatened them with instant death if they did not deposit their purses at the foot of the post. The farmers obeyed him in silent awe, and Faggus rode off with his booty.

He was once seized, while sitting in the alehouse at Simonsbath, but at his shrill whistle, his invaluable horse, having broken down the stable door, rushed into the house, and after seriously maltreating the enemies of his master with his hoofs and teeth, bore him off in triumph.

On another occasion he was recognized in Barnstaple and closely pursued to the bridge, where he was met by a party of constables who blockaded the other end. Seeing all hopes of escape by the road completely cut off, he boldly put his horse at the parapet of the bridge. This he cleared, and swam off to the very great disappointment of his numerous assailants, who had considered his capture as now quite certain.

Intelligence being received at Exford that Faggus was to pass through that village on a certain day, a number of men were stationed in the road to endeavour to seize him. They had not been long at their post before Faggus rode up in complete disguise. 'Pray, my good friends,' said he, 'may I ask for what purpose you are waiting here in such numbers?' On being answered that they were waiting for Faggus, he replied that he knew him well for a great rascal, and volunteered his services in assisting to take him.

After a little more conversation he asked what firearms they had; four or five guns were produced. He proposed that they should be discharged and reloaded, to secure their going off when required, as the dampness of the morning might have injured the priming.

This was agreed to, and when his advice had been taken and the guns were rendered temporarily useless, he produced his own pistols, and having declared his name and robbed his terrified adversaries, galloped away.

It being discovered on another occasion that Faggus had taken refuge in a house at Porlock, the whole of the inhabitants assembled; some seized the rusty arms which had long hung neglected over their chimneys, or been employed only in war against the timid wild fowl. Others armed themselves with scythes, pitchforks and other rustic weapons.

They surrounded the house in a formidable array, shouting aloud, 'Faggus is taken! Faggus is taken!' But they were mistaken; the door suddenly opened and he rushed forth mounted on his strawberry horse, dashing through the crowd. Regardless of the shots and blows aimed at him from all sides, he disappeared, leaving them astonished and confounded at his daring and good fortune.

He was at length captured in an alehouse at Exebridge, in the following manner. One of the officers disguised as an old beggar woman entered the tap room where Faggus was. With his usual kindness he ordered the supposed vagrant some food and liquor, and sat down near 'her'. At a preconcerted signal, the disguised constable, rising quickly, pulled the chair from under Faggus and was immediately joined by others who had been concealed in the room; they instantly fastened Faggus' feet and hoisted him up to the bacon rack.

The shrill whistle Faggus gave as was his custom when in difficulty was given in vain, for the poor horse had been shot in the stable at the very moment the attack was made upon his master.

All was now over with poor Faggus. He was tried and hanged at Taunton at the ensuing assizes.

Throughout his career not one act of cruelty was ever laid to his charge, whilst numerous are the acts of kindness and charity to the sick and the distressed, that are recorded of him. Like the celebrated Robin Hood, he seems to have taken from the rich to give to the poor, for it required but little to supply his own immediate wants, living as he did in the most frugal manner.

The ghost of the black dog

There are many tales of black dogs, and of the pack of Wisht or Wish Hounds, as they are known on Dartmoor, or Yeth Hounds on Exmoor, which hunt the wild hills, often with the demon huntsman close behind them. Here is just one.

A man having to walk from Princetown to Plymouth took the road across Roborough Down. He started at four o'clock from the Duchy Hotel, and as he walked at a good swinging pace, he hoped to cover the sixteen miles in about three hours and a half. It was a lovely December evening, cold and frosty, the stars and bright moon, giving enough light to enable him to see the roadway distinctly zigzagged across the moor. Not a friendly pony or a quiet Neddy crossed his path as he strode merrily onward whistling as he went. After a while, the desolation of the scene seemed to strike him, and he felt terribly alone among the boulders and huge masses of gorse which hemmed him in. On, on, he pressed, till he came to a village where a wayside inn tempted him to rest a while and have just one nip of something short to keep his spirits up.

Passing the reservoir beds he came out on an open piece of road, with a pine copse on his right. Just then he fancied he heard the pit-pat of feet gaining upon him. Thinking it was a pedestrian bound for Plymouth, he turned to accost his fellow traveller, but there was no one visible, nor were any footfalls then audible. Immediately on resuming his walk, pit-pat, pit-pat, fell the echoes of feet again.

And suddenly there appeared close to his right side an enormous dog, neither mastiff nor bloodhound, but what seemed to him to be a Newfoundland of immense size. Dogs were always fond of him, and he of them, so he took no heed of this, to him lovely, canine specimen. Presently he spoke to him, 'Well, doggie, what a beauty you are. How far are you going?' at the same time lifting his hand to pat him. Great was the man's astonishment to find no resisting substance, though the form was certainly there, for his hand passed right through the seeming body of the animal.

'Hullo, what's this?' said the bewildered traveller. As he spoke, the great glassy eyes gazed at him; then the beast yawned and from his throat issued a stream of sulphurous breath. Well, thought the man, I am in for it now! I'll just trudge on as fast as legs can carry me, without letting this queer customer think I am afraid of him. With heart beating madly and feet flying over the stony way, he hurried down the hill, the dog never for a moment leaving him or slackening its speed. They soon reached a crossway, not far from the fortifications, when suddenly the man was startled by a loud report, followed by a blinding flash as of lightning, which struck him senseless to the ground. At daybreak he was found by the driver of the mail-cart, lying unconscious in a ditch.

Tradition says that a foul murder was many years ago committed at this spot, and the victim's dog is doomed to traverse this road and kill every man he encounters, until the perpetrator of the deed has perished by his instrumentality. There are similar legends of the Black Dog throughout the county, and many wayside public houses have 'The Black Dog' for a sign.

'Tis only fayther

Once upon a time a gentleman set out on horseback to cross Dartmoor, at the breaking up of a long and hard frost when the roads were only just beginning to be passable. Now though the thaw had begun, it had not yet melted the snow drifts as much as he had expected; he progressed only slowly, and towards evening it began to freeze again.

The mighty tors, which seemed to grow larger and taller as he paced forward through the dusk, gradually became enveloped with vapour and mist. The traveller did not know what to do.

To reach Tavistock that night would be impossible, as a fresh snowstorm was fast falling in every direction, and would add even further dangers to the way. To stay out all night on the cold moor, without shelter or food, must be certain death, and yet where was shelter to be found?

In this dilemma there was no point in standing still, so he paced onward, and at length he saw at a distance a certain dark object but partially covered with snow. As he drew nearer, his heart revived, and his horse, which seemed to understand all the hopes and fears of his master, pricked up his ears and trotted on, or rather slid on, a little faster. The discovery which had thus rejoiced the heart of man and beast was not only that of the dark object, but also a thick smoke which rose like a stately column in the clear frosty air from its roof, and convinced them that what they now beheld must be a cottage.

He presently drew nigh and dismounted, and the rap that he gave with the butt-end of his whip upon the door was answered by an old woman, who invited him in. He entered and beheld a sturdy peasant who proved to be the old woman's son, who sat smoking his pipe over a cheerful and blazing peat fire. The traveller's needs were soon made known, for in those days a gentleman expected his requirements to be met with little question by any peasant. An old out-house with a litter of straw accommodated the horse which, it is not unlikely, ate up his bed for want of a better supper.

The traveller felt very hungry and wanted a bed. Though there was but one bed beside the old woman's in the house, the son, who seemed a surly fellow, promised to give it up for the convenience of the traveller, adding that he would himself sleep that night in the old settle by the chimney corner. The good dame busied herself in preparing such food as the house could afford for the stranger's supper, and at length he retired to rest. Neither the room nor the bedding were such as promised much comfort to a person accustomed to the luxuries of polished life, but as most things derive their value from comparison, even so did these mean lodgings, when he reflected how narrowly he had escaped perhaps being frozen to death that night on the bleak moor.

Before going to rest he had observed in the chamber a large oak chest; it was somewhat curious in form and ornament and had the appearance of being of great antiquity. He made some remarks upon it to the old woman when she had lighted him upstairs, in order to see that all things in his chamber were as comfortable for his repose as circumstances would admit. There was something, he thought, shy and odd about the woman when he remarked on the chest, and after she was gone he had half a mind to take a peep into it, but he forebore and went to bed as fast as he could.

He felt cold and miserable; and who in that condition can ever hope for a sound and refreshing sleep? His was neither the one nor the other, for the woman and the chest haunted him in his dream, and a hollow sound, as if from behind his bed head, started him out of his initial sleep. As he started up in bed, the first thing he saw was the old chest that had troubled him in his dreams. There it lay in the silvery silence of the moonlight, looking cold and white and, as connected with his dream, a provoking and even alarming object of his curiosity. And then he thought of the hollow sound, which had seemed to call him from his repose, and the old woman's odd manner when he had talked to her about the chest, and the reserve of her sturdy son, and in short the traveller's imagination supplied a thousand subjects of terror; indeed so active did it now become that it gave action even to the most inanimate things; for he looked and looked again, till he actually fancied the lid of the chest began to move slowly up before his eyes!

He could endure no more. Starting from his bed, he rushed forward, grasped the lid with trembling hands, and raised it up at once. Who shall speak his feelings when he beheld what that fatal chest now disclosed? – a human corpse, stiff and cold, lay before his sight! So much was he overcome with the horror of his feelings that it was with extreme difficulty that he could once more reach the bed.

How he passed the rest of the night he scarcely remembered; but one thought, one fear, possessed and agonised his whole soul. He was in the house of murderers! he was the next victim! there was no escape; for where, even if he left the chamber, at such an hour in such a night, where should he find shelter on the vast, frozen and desolate moor? He had no arms, he had no means of flight, for if plunder and murder were designed, he would not be allowed to pass out of the house while the young man (now, in his apprehension, a common trafficker in the blood of the helpless) slept in the only room below, and through which he must pass if he stirred from where he was.

To dwell on the thoughts and feelings of the traveller during that night of terror would be an endless task. Rather let me hasten to say that it was with the utmost thankfulness and not without some surprise that he found himself alive and undisturbed by any midnight assassin when the sun at last arose and threw the cheerful light of day across the monotonous desolation of the moor. He determined to hasten away, to pay liberally, but to avoid doing or saying anything to arouse suspicion.

On descending to the kitchen he found the old woman and her son busily employed in preparing no other fate for him than that of a good breakfast; and the son, who the night before was probably tired out with labour (and perhaps not all that pleased at the prospect of a night in the settle) had now lost what the gentleman had fancied to be a surly humour. He gave his guest a country salutation, hoped 'his honour' had found good rest, and proceeded to recommend the breakfast in the true spirit of honest hospitality; particularly praising the broiled bacon, as 'Mother was reckoned to have a particularly good hand at salting 'un in.'

Daylight, civility and broiled bacon the traveller now found to be the most excellent remedies against the terrors, both real and otherwise, of his imagination. The fright had disturbed his nerves, but the keen air of those high regions and the savoury smell of a fine smoking rasher, were great restoratives. Indeed so much did he feel reassured and elevated by the total extinction of all his personal fears that, just as the good woman was broiling him another rasher, he out with the secret of the chest, and let them know that he had been somewhat surprised by its contents, venturing in a friendly tone to ask for an explanation of so remarkable a circumstance.

'Bless your heart, your honour, 'tis nothing at all,' said the young man, ''tis only fayther!'

'Your father!' cried the traveller, 'What do you mean?'

'Why you see, your honour,' replied the peasant, 'the snaw being so thick, and making the roads so cledgey, like, when old fayther died two weeks agon, we couldn't carry 'un to Tavistock to bury 'un; so mother put 'un in the old box, and salted 'un in. Mother's a fine hand at salting 'un in.'

Need more be said of this sensitive traveller and his breakfast?

He now looked with horror at the smoking rasher, and fancied it nothing less than a slice of old fayther. He got up, paid for his lodging, saddled his horse, and quitting the house where surprise, terror, joy and disgust had all by turns so powerfully possessed him, he made his way through every impediment of snow and storm.

Never afterwards could he be prevailed upon to touch bacon.

Two stories of the barrows

In the words of Thomas Westcote (1630): A daily labouring man by the work of his hand and the sweat of his brow having gotten a little money, was desirous to have a place to rest himself in old age, and therefore invested it in some acres of waste land and began to build a house thereon, near a barrow named Broaken Burrow [in the parish of Challacombe, near Blackmore Gate] from which he fetched stones and earth to further his work. Having pierced into the bowels of the hillock, he found therein a little place, as if it had been a large oven, fairly, closely and strongly walled up; which comforted him much, hoping that there might be some treasure there hidden to maintain him more liberally and with less labour in his old years.

Wherewith encouraged, he plied his work earnestly until he had broken a hole through this wall, in the cavity of which he espied an earthen pot, which caused him to multiply his efforts until he might make the orifice large enough to take out the pot, which his earnest desire made not long a-doing. But as he thrust in his arm and fastened his arm thereon, he suddenly heard, or seemed to hear, the noise of the trampling of horses coming, as he thought, towards him, which caused him to forbear and arise from the place, fearing those coming would take his prize from him (for he had assured himself that it was treasure). But looking about every way to see what company this was, he saw neither horse nor man in view.

To the pot again he goes, and had the like success a second time; and yet, looking about, could see nothing. At the third time, he brought it out, and therein only a few ashes and bones, as if they had been of children or the like. But the man, whether by the fear (which yet he denied) or other cause which I cannot comprehend, in very short time after lost the sense both of sight and hearing, and in less than three months consuming, died.

The innkeeper's daughter

When Parliament's troopers were in Tavistock during the Civil War, knowing that the innkeeper at the King's Arms was a royalist, they determined that his wine should not be used to drink healths to the king. The best way to prevent this seemed to be to wash it down their own throats, so that not a drop of ungodly wine should remain if the royalists retook the town.

But they started by clearing out all the food upstairs, which gave time for the innkeeper's daughter to form a plan. She was in the last stages of tuberculosis, or 'consumption', and of a wasted and ghastly appearance. She resolutely snatched up a white tablecloth and, thus attired, stole downstairs and took her post in the dingy confines of an old wine-cellar, at the extremity of a long, narrow, congested and ominously dark passage.

When she heard them making their way down the steps, she groaned a groan and stood still. The corporal who headed the marauding party stared towards the sound, and his eye caught the pale, thin, white and shadowy figure that, in a motionless attitude, stood with upraised and menacing hand at the back of the cellar.

'What the devil is that?' said one of the fellows.

'Devil or no devil, I will send a shot at the white mark,' said another. He raised his pistol and took a steady aim at the inn-keeper's daughter. She neither moved nor spoke, such was her resolution.

'Do not fire,' said the corporal. 'The figure mocks thine attempts; do not strive with spirit, for yonder thing is neither flesh nor blood. Let us begone from this place, or something may happen.'

'Now I look again,' said the trooper, 'I see it is a ghost. The Lord have mercy upon us! I will sing a psalm!'

At hearing this the ghost was moved, and making as if she would advance upon the whole party, she sent every mother's son of them flying in fright. Up the steps they ran, much faster than they had descended.

The cellar escaped rifling; the house was instantly abandoned; they didn't even stay to collect the booty they had already gathered above stairs.

The Parson and the Clerk

Near Dawlish stand, out in the sea, two rocks of red sand-stone conglomerate, bearing these names. They are not the originals, which have long since worn away, but the story which attached itself to them was too good to be lost, so replacement rocks were found! Here is their story.

The Bishop of Exeter was sick unto death at Dawlish. An ambitious priest frequently rode with his clerk to make anxious enquiries after the condition of the dying bishop. It is whispered that this priest had great hopes of occupying the bishop's throne in Exeter cathedral.

The clerk was usually the priest's guide but somehow or other, on a particularly stormy night, he lost the road and they were wandering over Haldon. Excessively angry was the priest, and very provoking was the clerk. He led his master this way and that way, yet still they were on the elevated country of Haldon. At length the priest exclaimed in a great rage, 'I would rather have the Devil for a guide than you.'

Presently the clatter of a horse's hoofs was heard behind them and a peasant rode up on a moor pony. The priest told of his problem, and the peasant volunteered to guide them. On rode peasant, priest and clerk, and soon they were at Dawlish. The night was tempestuous, the ride had quickened the appetite of the priest, and he was wet through. Therefore, when his peasant friend asked him to supper, as they approached an old, ruined house, through the windows of which bright lights were shining, there was no hesitation in accepting the invitation.

There were a host of friends gathered together, a strange, wild-looking bunch of men. But as the tables were laden with substantial dishes, and black-jacks of beer or cider were standing thick around, the parson, and the clerk too, soon became friends with all.

They ate and drank, and became most irreligiously uproarious. The parson sang hunting songs, and songs in praise of a certain old gentleman with whom a priest should not have maintained any acquaintance. These in particular were highly appreciated, and every man joined loudly in the chorus. Night wore away, and at last news was brought that the bishop was dead. This appeared to rouse up the parson, who was only too eager to set to work to secure his ambition. So master and man mounted their horses, and bade adieu to their hilarious friends.

They were at the door of the mansion – yet somehow or other the horses did not seem disposed to move. They were whipped and spurred, but to no purpose.

'The devil's in the horses,' said the priest.

'I b'lieve he is,' said the clerk.

'Devil or no devil, they shall go,' said the parson, cutting his horse madly with his heavy whip.

There was a roar of unearthly laughter.

The priest looked round. His drinking friends were all turned to demons, wild with glee, and the peasant guide was an arch little devil, looking on with a marvellously curious twinkle in his eyes. The noise of waters was around them; and now the priest discovered that the mansion had disappeared, and that waves beat heavy on his horse's flanks, and rushed over the smaller horse of his man.

Repentance was too late.

In the morning following this stormy night, two horses were found straying on the sands near Dawlish; and clinging with the grasp of death to two rocks, were found the parson and the clerk. There today stand the rocks to which the devil has given the forms of the tall parson, and his clerk standing below and in front of him, an enduring monument to all generations.

The gallant Mrs Partington

Sydney Smith, a reformist politician of the early nineteenth century, made the following comment on the attempts of the House of Lords to prevent reform of the electoral system, especially the elimination of 'rotten boroughs' from which peers benefited.

'I do not mean to be disrespectful but the attempt of the Lords to stop the progress of reform reminds me very forcibly of the great storm at Sidmouth, and of the conduct of the excellent Mrs Partington on that occasion. In the winter of 1824 there set in a great flood upon that town – the tide rose to an incredible height

– the waves rushed in upon the houses, and everything was threatened with destruction.

'In the midst of this sublime and terrible storm, Dame Partington, who lived upon the beach, was seen at the door of her house with mop and pattens, trundling her mop, squeezing out the sea water, and vigorously pushing away the Atlantic Ocean. The Atlantic was roused. Mrs Partington's spirit was up. But I need not tell you the contest was unequal. The Atlantic Ocean beat Mrs Partington. She was excellent with a slop or a puddle, but she should not have meddled with a tempest.'

Drake scares the demons

When Sir Francis Drake was building a mansion out of the stones of Buckland Abbey, some supernatural force removed them to a great distance. This happened twice, before Sir Francis lost patience and determined to watch for his mysterious enemy. So he climbed into a tree. At midnight a troop of little devils ascended from the earth and with much merriment proceeded to raze the walls and remove the stones as before.

Once more the workmen built the walls and that night Sir Francis dressed himself in white and again mounted into his leafy shelter. Up came the devils as before, but when they approached the tree Sir Francis worked his arms and called 'Kikkeriki!' with all his might. Even devils have nerves, and this was too much. They fled in dismay, and so the mansion was built.

Smuggler's Leap

On the road from Lynton towards the hamlet of Martinhoe, at a point where it most closely approaches the sea, is a chasm called 'the Smuggler's Leap'. Many years ago, when running contraband was a regular part of Devon life, a smuggler was riding fast over these cliffs, pursued by a king's officer.

The exciseman had a better horse, and gained rapidly on his quarry. As pursuer and pursued drew abreast of the chasm, they were neck and neck and the smuggler swerved to avoid the exciseman's grasp. The movement was too much for his tired horse, which stumbled and with a wild snort went over the brink. But the smuggler did not fall alone. As he felt himself going, he clutched wildly at his enemy, and they rolled into the abyss together. It is said their bodies were discovered by seaweed gatherers 'locked together in a vice-like grip which had hurled them to eternity.'

The highwayman monk

Not far from Dawlish, at a place variously called Lidwell, Lithewell or Lady-Well, there dwelt a monk with a mighty appetite for good food, and without the means to enjoy it. His remedy was to assume nightly the dress of a wayfarer and to trudge the roads demanding 'Your money or your life,' from wealthy travellers. By day he would lure women to his chapel and, after robbing and murdering them, throw their bodies down a disused well.

After the suppression of the monasteries, and of his chapel, the well was found to contain a large number of human bones, which it was affirmed were those of women and young children. The shadowy forms of the women are sometimes seen hovering over this spot, while the wailing cries of children fill the air.

For once there is some historical evidence to support the legend. Robert of Middelcote, priest, was found guilty on 28 March 1328 of raping Agnes, daughter of Roger the Miller, and of burgling Robert Rossel's house and robbing Walter Scoria and others on the highway between Teignmouth and Haldon Hill.

The cannon ball marriage

A lady of the Drake family of Ashe House was betrothed to a sailor but broke her troth during his absence on some distant voyage, and chose another bridegroom. The wedding feast had begun and all was going on quite cheerfully, when the door opened without hands, and everyone turned to see who was coming in. For a moment nothing entered; but when the attention of the whole company had been roused, a cannon ball made its appearance rolling gently along the ballroom floor. It rolled on steadily and slowly until it reached the feet of the faithless bride, when it stopped and rooted itself so firmly to the ground that the united strength of those present could not make it budge.

It was clear that this remarkable event was a portent demanding close attention, and the lady very wisely interpreted it as a gentle hint that she was using the absent sailor rather badly. It was not too late to repent; which she accordingly did, sending her new lover about his business, and herself waiting for him who had a better right to her.

In Somerset, the same tale was told of Combe Sydenham house, where the 'cannonball' was long preserved. It was most probably a meteorite.

The Devil's little joke

One night a moorman was riding home from Widecombe Fair. He had made money and had then had something to keep out the cold, for the night promised to be one of tempest. As he started on his homeward way, the moon shone out occasionally between the whirling masses of thick vapour. The horse knew the way perhaps better than his master, and they had crossed the great ridge of Hameldon and were mounting towards a circle of upright stones – reputedly a Druid circle, where the stones are said to dance on Christmas Eve – when he heard a sound that startled him, a horn; and then past him swept without a footfall a pack of black dogs.

The moorman was not much frightened – he had taken too much Dutch courage for that – and when, a minute after, the black hunter came up, he shouted to him, 'Hey, huntsman, what sport? Give us some of your game.'

'Take that,' answered the hunter, and flung him something which the man caught and held in his arms. Then the mysterious hunter passed on. An hour elapsed before the moorman reached his home. As he jogged on, he wondered what sort of game he had been given. It was too large to be a hare, too small for a deer. Not once since his meeting with the hunter had the moon flashed forth. Now that he was at his door, he swung himself heavily from his horse and, still carrying the game, called for a lantern.

The light was brought. With one hand the fellow took it, then raised it to throw a ray on that which he held in his arm – the game hunted and won by the black rider of the moor. It was his own baby, dead and cold.

Cutty Dyer

The River Yeo at Ashburton is liable to 'freshets' or flash floods. At night, before the bridge was built, it was crossed on stepping stones, which depended on nerve and sobriety. The task was made much more difficult by an ogre called Cutty Dyer, who lay in wait for drunkards crossing the stream. He was described by people who saw him as being very tall, standing in the water to his waist, with red eyes as large as saucers, endeavouring to pull them into the water. When the stream was bridged, Cutty remained only to frighten little children into obedience, and he disappeared altogether when the streets were lit.

The night of the long knives

The Danes at one time held Hembury Castle, and the area around Buckfastleigh and Holne. They were only a raiding party, without their womenfolk, and they got hold of Saxon women when they could. They were such strong fighters that the Saxons could not drive them out, and a number of Saxon women decided to achieve what their men could not. They let themselves be 'surprised' and taken by the Danes, and that night at a given signal each one cut the throat of the man who lay with her. The Saxon men made an attack at the same time, so the castle was taken, which is how the Danes were got rid of at last.

'It is your choice to believe these stories or no.'
Thomas Westcote, *c*1630

THE END